Christmas Magic

Jason R. Van Pelt

Copyright © 2022 Jason R. Van Pelt

All rights reserved. No part of this book may be reproduced or transmitted in any form or by any means, electronic or mechanical, including photocopying, recording or by any information storage and retrieval system without permission in writing from the publisher.

J.R.V.P.—Madison, WI
ISBN: 978-1-7371572-2-9
Library of Congress Control Number: 2022922934
Title:*Christmas Magic*
Author: Jason R. Van Pelt
Digital distribution | 2022
 Paperback | 2022

This is a work of fiction. The characters, names, incidents, places, and dialogue are products of the author's imagination, and are not to be construed as real.

Dedication

Wishing a very merry happy holiday season to all.

Mother Vixen and Father Blitzen are the reindeer parents of Roxanne the green nose.
Mom Cupid and Dad Comet are the reindeer parents of Rudolf the red nose o' rose.

Dancer, Prancer, Dasher, and Donder are too part of the wintry sleighing team.
All of them working together with the Clauses Santa & Sandy for thy Christmas dream.

The silver elf Tinsel thinks of everybody and everything therefore creating a wellbeing for herself.
She's seen among the North Pole believing in saving the environment & animals of the arctic shelf.

'Tis a fine silver lining the way climate change can cause the world to behave strangely ever so inclining.
Reclining glaciers and ice caps are melting erewhile ocean levels are rising amid islands declining.

Tinsel braves the elements marching onward unto the snowbelt like a real life elf of a shelf on a mission.
To save the polar bears and prevent them from becoming extinct withal that Christmassy permission.

10

Creating awareness to the igloo tribes, ice caves, Claus city, and every outpost hereby her festive fairness.
She passes out brochures as well as gives lectures toward all those northern inhabitants of careness.

Whilst ongoing one of her adventures Tinsel is swept away by a whipper wind falling through the cracks.
She descends deeply downwards in a cavern hundreds of yards underneath the surface sans any feet tracks.

Luckily her sled of food supplies fell inwards in this icy crevice alongside her yet getting out is a doubt.
Her shout of help is unheard ergo she feels forgotten alike an egg gone rotten which initiates her pout.

Days become weeks, months, and years of lonely tears as she succumbs to desocialization so stark.
Hark! Often said that an elf without anyone else loses its' humble spark of happiness thus turns dark.

Something catches her attention similar to a twinkling star from the lonely iced abyss very drastic.
A name of "Sandy May Claus" is written onto the handle of a candle shaped Christmas wand o' magic.

Erstwhile Roxanne & Rudolf are educating schools of elves on toy safety that will spread to all people.
Small pieces and balloons could turn into choking hazards while sharps are as pointy as a steeple.

Parents must be mindful on the timing to give a present requiring the maturity of an age limit.
Courageously canoeing carefully and also kayaking has prerequisites of a license or permit.

Safety around water shall rescue lives in the manner Lifeguards do as well as snug life jackets.
They discuss seatbelts, staying hydrated, and dressing in layers walking within snowshoe rackets.

Green & red lights signal to traffic either airborne, seagoing, or an earthbound ramification.
Plastics should be disposed of quickly and properly to avoid airway obstruction n' asphyxiation.

Dark elf Tinsel made it back to the North Pole outskirts and to her it seems festivities have continued.
She has some troubling thoughts that nobody was even missing her hence what she has viewed.

Snowmen wearing hats, scarves, jelly buttons, carrot noses, molasses pantaloons, & licorice smiles.
Ice sculptures of dragons, mammoths, vultures, penguins, lions, and cultures across snowy piles.

The dark elf Tinsel starts abusing the Christmas wand she located by performing darkened spells.
Casting snowmen into abominable yetis and possessing an ice dragon with scales slick as hair gels.

She's undoubted since her judgement is shrouded laying the North Pole under siege and lockdown.
The arctic now surrounded wherefore Santa, Sandy, & company stay grounded in a saddened frown.

Tinsel the dark elf aims to make the entire world feel abandoned the way she felt beneath that snowbelt.
From lavishing to languishing she is thwarting the delivery of the Christmastide presents being dealt.

Alas! Are we hanging on by a thread of a rope, down to the last drop of soap, the answer is nope.
Lo! A green and red glow of Roxanne The Antarctican as well as Rudolf The Arctican shines hope.

After an epic standstill, a freeze frame if you will, comes a sudden epiphany of whom it is they see.
Standing there in front of Roxanne & Rudolf looking lost howbeit found in a sense of familiarity.

Resembled Tinsel, can this really be, she was featured daily in a newspaper inside a missed elf testimonial.
The whole North Pole longed for her return and during the meantime created a "Tinsel Town" memorial.

Assembled search parties led by Roxanne and Rudolf combed the arctic everyday aligning chakras.
Tinsel reverts to her silver self-beginning at her hair, head, neck, heart, stomach, hips, and legs of genres.

Tinsel hands Sandy Claus the wand and that teeter reminds her she cares about undoing her errors.
All the snow creatures endure a reversal and Christmas is given right on time to heiresses & heirs!

Also by Jason R. Van Pelt

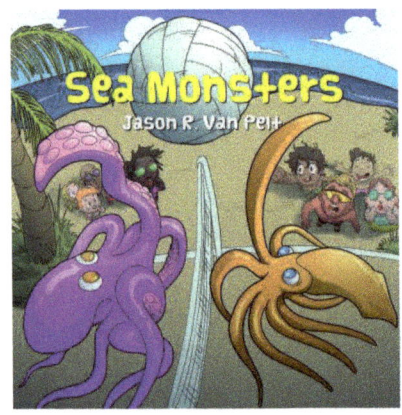

www.ingramcontent.com/pod-product-compliance
Lightning Source LLC
Chambersburg PA
CBHW051320110526
44590CB00031B/4413